Illustrated Workbook

For

Freedom from Your Inner Critic: A Self Therapy Approach

Bonnie Weiss, LCSW

Illustrations by Karen Donnelly

Pattern Systems Books
140 Marina Vista Ave.
Larkspur, CA 94939
415 924-5200
www.patternsystembooks.com

ISBN: 978-0-9855937-7-3
ISBN: 9780985593773

Illustrated Workbook
for
Freedom from Your Inner Critic

Bonnie Weiss, LCSW

This is the illustrated workbook for *Freedom from Your Inner Critic* by Bonnie Weiss and Jay Earley. The book is intended to help people process the basic concepts of the **IFS model and our Inner Critic work.** It is a companion workbook and is not intended as a complete course in either Internal Family Systems (IFS) or the workings of the inner critic. It is designed to provide supplemental learning opportunities through visual representations, thought-provoking questions, imagery exercises, and artistic opportunities.

This Workbook can be used by therapists, counselors, or teachers familiar with the IFS model. Classes, groups, or individuals can interact with the concepts through discussion and personal sharing.

If you are an individual with no prior familiarity with IFS, I suggested that you use either *Freedom from Your Inner Critic* or *Self Therapy* by Jay Earley along with this workbook to flesh out the material.

Basic Concepts Covered:

> ➢   Seeing the difference between blended and unblended parts.
> ➢   Becoming curious about an Inner Critic part from the position of Self.
> ➢   Exploring a part's motivation and befriending it.
> ➢   Illustrating witnessing and unburdening.
> ➢   Seven types of Inner Critics
> ➢   Seven types of Inner Champions

Internal Family Systems Therapy (IFS) is a new, cutting-edge form of psychotherapy developed by psychologist Richard Schwartz, which has been spreading rapidly across the country in the last decade. IFS is not only extremely effective with a wide variety of psychological issues, but it is also user-friendly and lends itself especially well to self-therapy. IFS makes it easy to comprehend the complexity of your psyche. *Freedom from Your Inner Critic* shows you how to use IFS to transform your Inner

Critic. My hope is that this illustrated workbook will support this process and be a supplement to our written text.

The Inner Critic: Many people go through periods of believing there is something inherently wrong with them. It can be very helpful to discover that this low self-esteem is coming from a part of us called the Inner Critic. It is often a surprise and a relief to discover that these feelings of depression, shame, and worthlessness are a result of negative messages sent by this part which is only trying to help in a distorted way. An Inner Critic usually takes on the burden of trying to protect a child part that was not fully accepted for being him or herself. The Critic's efforts are intended to prevent continued hurt, shame or rejection by making us more acceptable to our external social environment.

An Inner Critic may:

> Evaluate and judge our feelings and behavior and sometimes our core self.
> Tell us what we should and shouldn't do.
> Criticize us for not meeting its expectations or the expectations of significant people in our lives.
> Doubt our capacity to achieve success or happiness.
> Make us feel guilty or ashamed about ourselves or something we have done.

Our focus on the Inner Critic has led us to delineate seven different flavors of Inner Critics. We find that our descriptions and illustrations of them allow people to universalize their own experience and often gain deeper insight into the actions and motivations of their personal Critic. Seeing it through this vantage point can bring to light subtle dynamics that can be explored in personal inquiry and therapy sessions.

Even though we use categories of parts, such as Inner Critic, Criticized Child, and Inner Defender, please remember that each person's parts are unique. We encourage people to discover the unique characteristics and attributes of each of their parts and call them by whatever names seem right. The ideas put forth here are not to put parts into boxes, but to suggest possibilities that may lead to deeper understanding.

The Inner Champion: Our work suggests that we can each develop a aspect of the Self that we call the Inner Champion. This is a magic bullet for dealing with the negative impact of the Inner Critic. Since we have outlined seven types of Inner Critics, we have also identified seven corresponding types of Inner Champions. Each of these Champions has a number of important capacities:

> The strength to set boundaries on attacks from the Inner Critic.
> The capacity to nurture and comfort parts that are at the effect of the Inner Critic.
> An intuitive ability to hold a wider vision and see things from a broader perspective.
> The capacity to plan and take effective action.

We have found that helping our clients to bring forth these capacities sustains the healing work done around the Inner Critic.

We All Have Parts

Parts are like little people inside us. They each
try to help us in the their own special way.

A part can be a role you play, a way you feel, or a way that you behave
or think about yourself.

What would you name some of the parts on this page?

_____   _____

_____   _____

_____   _____

_____   _____

Parts in the Outside World

Some parts help us manage our lives. They interact with others to help us get things done, take care of ourselves, and have relationships.

Name some of the parts on this page. _____
_____
_____

Name some of **your** parts that deal with the outside world.
_____
_____

How do you feel when they are present? _____
_____
_____
_____

Parts in the Inside World

Some parts take care of our inner world. They can be voices in our heads, bodily sensations, or emotional feelings. Sometimes they are kind and supportive, and sometimes they can be critical or bossy.

Take a moment and close your eyes. Listen inside. What do you hear? (For example, "I am a good person, I deserve love," or "There's something wrong with me, I'm not perfect enough," or "Who do you think you are to dream *that* dream?")

Write what you hear inside you._____
_____
_____

How does it make you feel to hear these words? _____
_____
_____

Inner Critic Parts

Inner Critic parts are voices in our head or feelings about ourselves that make us feel bad, imperfect, or unworthy. They have ideas about who we are or how we should be that can limit and constrain us and cause self-doubt.

How do you experience your Inner Critic? An internal voice you hear? A general feeling about yourself? A sense that you are wrong or bad?

_____

_____

What are the words that you hear? Or the beliefs you hold about yourself?

_____

_____

_____

_____

_____

Childhood Origins

Sometimes things happen in childhood that
hurt us and make us feel bad about ourselves.

Can you remember a time when you were younger when something
happened to make you feel bad about yourself?

_____

_____

_____

What **current** feelings or beliefs about yourself come from that time?
(For example, "I believe that I can't ask for what I want.")

_____

_____

_____

_____

Inner Critic's Motivation

You better look perfect or they won't love you!

Inner Critic parts are Protector parts, and like all parts, they have a positive motivation. They are trying to help you in some way. The Critic might be trying to stop you from doing something that caused you to be shamed or rejected in the past. It might be trying to make sure you are loved and approved of. Or it might think it is keeping you safe by making you small and invisible.

What kind of protection did you need when you were young? Did you want to be invisible, not make mistakes or to always fit in?_____

_____

_____

_____

What do you think your Inner Critic is trying to protect you from now?

_____

_____

What Does Your Inner Critic Look Like?

When you close your eyes and hear the voice of your Inner Critic, do you get a picture of what it looks like?
It could be an animal; a figure from TV, the movies, or mythology; or a feeling expressed in colored lines.

Draw this critic in the box. Remember that there is no right or wrong. These are your personal images.

The Self Is Who You Truly Are

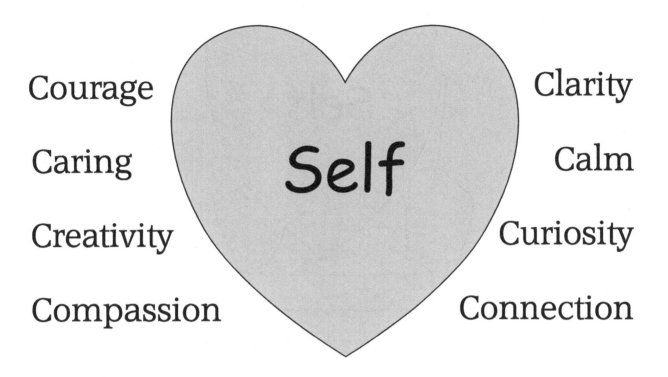

Courage

Caring

Creativity

Compassion

Self

Clarity

Calm

Curiosity

Connection

The Self is the big, spacious place in and around us. It manifests the higher human capacities.

How do you feel when you are in Self?

Take a deep breath. Close your eyes. Feel your feet on the ground or put your hand on your belly. Imagine that you are filled with any one of the Self qualities: courage, caring, creativity, compassion, clarity, calm, curiosity, or connection.

Now feel into your body. What do you notice? _____
_____
_____
_____

The Seat of Consciousness

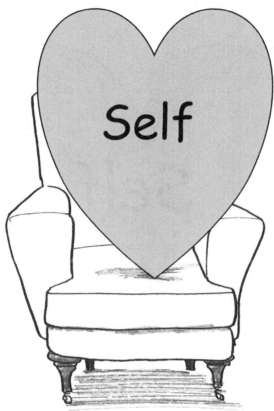

The Self is the natural occupant of the Seat of Consciousness when none of our parts have stepped in or gotten in the way.

Imagine what it would be like to live your life from this place of Self?

What would you feel? _____

_____

_____

What would you do differently? _____

_____

_____

What would it look like to others?_____

_____

_____

Blending: When a Part Takes Over the Seat of Consciousness

Parts can take over the Seat of Consciousness so that it is hard to find the Self. Then you relate to others from a reactive place.

Name a part of you that often takes over your Seat of Consciousness.
_____
_____

What does your body feel like when this part is there?_____
_____
_____

What emotions do you feel?_____
_____

How do you act when it is there?_____
_____

Unblending:
Relating to a Part from Self

You (as Self) can be separate from the part so that you can be curious about it and get to know it.

Can you imagine what it would be like to be separate from your part?

_____

_____

From this place of Self, can you be curious about it?_____

_____

_____

_____

Criticized Child Parts

You are a lazy, useless child.

You can't do anything right.

Sometimes when the Inner Critic is present, you feel like a hurt, weak, sad, rejected child. This is because you are blended with an exile part that we call the Criticized Child.

Think of a time when you were feeling really bad about yourself. What did you think was true about you? (For example, I'm not smart. I'll never amount to anything. My body is ugly.)_____
_____
_____

What feelings do you feel (For example, sad, hopeless, depressed.)?
_____
_____

What do you feel in your body (For example, heavy, sleepy, dense)?_____
_____

Blended with the Inner Critic
and the Criticized Child

Sometimes we can be blended with both the Inner Critic and the Criticized Child at the same time. The Self is hidden, and we cannot access its strength and compassion.

Can you think of a time when you could feel both the feelings of the Criticized Child and the Critic? (For example, I was procrastinating on finishing a paper. I felt stupid and scared, AND, at the same time, angry at myself for not starting sooner._____

_____

_____

What feelings or thoughts change when you understand this idea?

_____

_____

_____

The Self Is Curious
About Critic

You can find a nurturing part inside you to
have compassion for the Criticized Child.

What would your Criticized Child like to hear from a nurturing part of you?
_____
_____

What questions would you like to ask your Inner Critic?
_____
_____
_____

What Does Your Nurturing Aspect Look Like?

Imagine that you could harness the power of love and bring it into yourself to nurture those parts of you that have been hurt in the past. Close your eyes and feel what that would be like in your body to receive that love.

What words would you hear? _____

Allow an image to develop that represents that nurturing part.

Draw this image in the box. Remember, you can't make mistakes. These are expressions of whatever is true for you.

Getting To Know the Critic and Developing a Trusting Relationship With It

The next six pages illustrate this concept.

Sarah's Inner Critic

Sarah's Critic says mean things to her and makes
her feel as if she doesn't have a right to exist.
She feels as if it is trying to crush her life force.

What do you imagine that Sarah's Inner Critic is saying to her that makes
her feel so bad? _____

_____

_____

What do you think her feelings are? _____

_____

Inner Defender Parts

Sarah has a part inside of her that defends her against her Inner Critic. It takes over the Seat of Consciousness.

What do you imagine that Sarah's Inner Defender is saying to her Inner Critic to try to make it back off? _____
_____
_____

How do you think the Inner Critic responds? _____
_____
_____
_____

Unblending from the Inner Defender

Though Sarah appreciates that her Inner Defender is fighting for her, she knows this kind of inner combat isn't an effective way to handle the Inner Critic. Its just two parts fighting. She wants to be in Self and be curious about both parts.

What do you think Sarah wants to know about her Inner Critic (For example, when it came into being, what it was trying to protect her from, what it really wants for her)?_____

_____

_____

_____

_____

Befriending the Critic

When Sarah began to develop a relationship with her Inner Critic, it calmed down. It was grateful for the attention and became less threatening.

What did the Inner Critic say about why it acted the way it did? _____
_____
_____
_____

How do you think Sarah felt hearing this? _____
_____
_____

The Child Inside

Sarah's Critic is really just a little kid trying to handle a job that is too big for her. It is trying hard to protect her from harmful things happening to her **now** that probably did happen when she was little.

What do you think little Sarah was thinking when she put on the monster costume and began acting mean to Sarah? _____

_____

_____

_____

What do you think she was feeling?_____

_____

Nurturing The Child Critic

When Sarah sees that the little girl was just
scared she wants to comfort and nurture her.

What do you think this nurturing Self is saying to little Sarah? _____
_____
_____

How do you think little Sarah is feeling now? _____
_____
_____
_____

Getting to Know the Critic
Unburdening the Criticized Child

The next six pages illustrate this concept.

George's Inner Critic

This is why I push you.

George's Critic tells him, "I push you to work hard so that you will succeed and your boss will be happy with you."

What do you imagine George's Inner Critic is saying to him to make him work so hard? _____
_____
_____
_____

The Critic's Motivation

George's Critic tells him, "I am afraid that if I don't push you, you will be lazy and get in trouble with your boss."

What do you think George's Inner Critic is afraid will happen if he is lazy?

_____

_____

_____

_____

_____

Befriending the Critic

George now understands his Critic and
it trusts him, so they can work together.

How do you think George and his Inner Critic are each feeling now?

_____

_____

_____

_____

Witnessing The Critic's Childhood Origins

George's Criticized Child shows him a memory of his father's harsh criticism. This caused the Critic to take on its burden of protecting the Child by pushing him to work hard and avoid disapproval.

How is little boy is feeling as his father checks his homework? _____
_____
_____

How do you think the boy is feeling when George listens to his story?
_____
_____
_____

Identifying a Burden and Releasing It

The Criticized Child shows George the stone of hurt in
his heart that is a result of his father's disapproval.
George helps him release this burden by burying the stone.

What do you think it is like for the little boy to have help taking out that
stone of sadness and burying it? _____
_____
_____
_____
_____

The Unburdened Child and Critic

Burying the stone unburdens the little boy's pain so he now feels whole and happy. George's Critic sees this and can stop pushing him.

What do you think the boy is feeling now? _____
_____
_____

What is the critic feeling now that he sees the boy transformed?_____
_____
_____
_____

The Seven Types of Critics

Perfectionist

Molder

Guilt Tripper

Underminer

Taskmaster

Controller

Destroyer

Perfectionist Inner Critic

No! No! No! That's
not good enough!

Some Critics try to protect you by
making sure you do everything perfectly.

Do you have a Perfectionist Critic telling you to be perfect? _____
_____

What does it say to you? _____
_____
_____

Controller Inner Critic

You're disgusting!

Some protectors make you feel bad about what you eat, use, or drink, or how your body looks.

Do you have an Controller Inner Critic that makes you feel bad about your body or the things you eat, use, or drink? _____

_____

What does it say to you? _____

_____

_____

Underminer Inner Critic

Don't even bother. You'll never be good enough.

Some protector parts keep you from trying new things and following your dreams.

Do you have an Underminer Critic that tries to stop you from attempting new things and makes you doubt if you can be who you want to be?

_____

What does it say to you? _____

_____

_____

Guilt Tripper Inner Critic

You're bad. You don't deserve forgiveness.

Some protector parts make you feel bad
about what you have done and who you are.

Do you have a Guilt Tripper Critic that makes you feel bad about yourself
for something you have done or some way that you are? _____
_____

What does it say to you? _____
_____
_____

Molder Inner Critic

I'll show you the right way to be.

Some protector parts tell you how you should be:
how to look, how to think, and how to do things.

Do you have a Molder Inner Critic that tells you how you should look,
think and act, based on who other people think you should be? _____
_____
_____

What does it say to you? _____
_____
_____

Taskmaster Inner Critic

This Critic pushes you to work hard and is never satisfied that you have done enough.

Do you have a Taskmaster Inner Critic that pushes you to work harder and harder and doesn't want you to rest or take time for yourself?_____

_____

What does it say to you? _____

_____
_____

Destroyer Inner Critic

Some protector parts make you feel as if you don't
have the right to exist. They try to crush your life force.

Do you have a Destroyer Inner Critic that makes you feel so bad about
yourself that you think you're not entitled to anything?_____
_____

What does it say to you?_____
_____
_____

Role of the Inner Champion

1. **Boundary Setting with the Critic**

Your Inner Champion can set limits on your Inner Critic when necessary. This can create space and allow you to feel into yourself and take stock. It can make statements to your Inner Critic such as the following:

Your judgments aren't helpful.
Now is not a good time for this.
Your judgments are making things more difficult for me.

2. **Nurturing**

Your Inner Champion can make supportive, nurturing statements to you that help you to accept and appreciate yourself. For example:

I completely accept you, no matter what.
I love you.
I care about you.

3. **Guidance**

Your Inner Champion can make encouraging statements to help guide you on your way and support you to move ahead in your life. These statements might sound like this:

You can trust yourself.
Your struggles just represent where you are now in your growth.
You can do it.

4. **Action Planning**

Your Inner Champion can make suggestions to help you plan actions you need to take. It can say:

You have the right to take your time and do things at your own pace.
Congratulations on accomplishing that step.
You can overcome any obstacle in your path.

Sources for the Inner Champion

One source for your Inner Champion is the experiences you have had in your life from the people, real or imagined, you have felt, seen or been heard by. They are the people who have touched you in a special way and seen you for who you really are. They have reached out a helping hand or supported you when you were down.

Perhaps the model for your Inner Champion is a family member, a teacher, a coach, or a friend's parent.

Name some of the people in your life who have seen you, reached out to you, or touched you deeply. _____

_____

_____

_____

_____

We can also look for Champion sources in figures from literature, the arts, TV, movies, or mythology. You can access the Champion's wisdom from people you admired as they lived their lives with integrity. You can remember people who were kind and supportive to others,as well as people who held visions for themselves and those they loved.

Who have been your Champions?

List people real or imagined who possess the qualities of vision, strength, truth, gentleness, generosity and practicality that you admire.

_____

_____

_____

_____

_____

_____

The Seven Champions

Perfectionist

Controller

Underminer

Guilt Tripper

Molder

Taskmaster

Destroyer

The Inner Champion is the magic bullet that helps you deal with the negative impact of the Inner Critic.

Perfectionist Inner Champion

From a larger perspective you are fine just the way you are.

Your Perfectionist Inner Champion has a larger vision of things. It sees you as being fine just the way you are.

What would you like to hear your Inner Champion to say to you that would make you feel OK about not being perfect all the time?_____

_____

_____

How would you feel if you heard those words? _____

_____

Controller Inner Champion

I'll help you with balance flexibility and moderation.

Your Controller Inner Champion supports you to feel good about your body and teaches you how to care for it.

What would you like to hear from your Inner Champion to make you feel just fine about your body? _____
_____
_____
_____

What kind of help would you like from your Inner Champion in taking care of yourself? _____
_____
_____
_____

Underminer Champion

You have what it takes to follow your dreams.

STAGE DOOR

inner Champion

Your Underminer Inner Champion supports
you to try new things and be visible in the world.

What would you like to hear your Inner Champion say to give you
confidence in trying new things or following your dreams?_____
_____
_____
_____

How would you feel if you heard those words?_____
_____

Guilt Tripper Inner Champion

I'll help you have the strength to live by your own truth.

The Guilt Tripper Inner Champion helps you look at the truth about what you did or who you are, without making you feel bad about yourself.

What would you like to hear your Inner Champion say to you to make sure you feel OK about who you are and feel better about things you have done? _____

_____

_____

How would you feel if you heard those words? _____

_____

Molder Inner Champion

You're free to be yourself!

Your Molder Inner Champion helps
you be free to be who you really are.

What would you like your Inner Champion to say to you that would help
you feel free to figure out who you really are? _____
_____
_____
_____

How would you feel if you heard those words? _____
_____

Taskmaster Inner Champion

I'll support you to do it with ease and confidence.

This Inner Champion enhances your capacity to accomplish things with inner support.

What would you like to hear your Inner Champion say that would help you to work with more ease, confidence, and balance in your life?

_____
_____
_____

How would you feel if you heard those words? _____
_____

Destroyer Inner Champion

The Destroyer Inner Champion is a loving part
that makes you safe and feel good about yourself.

What would you like to hear your Inner Champion say to you that would
make you feel safe and loved and happy about who you are. What words
make you feel warm inside?_____

_____

_____

_____

_____

Draw Your Inner Champion

You can have one Inner Champion or many. It can be human, animal, mythological, or just an energetic swirl of color. When you go inside and ask, "What is the perfect support that I need to deal with the issues in my life at this moment?" what do you see?

Draw that image and, if you like, write any words that come to you as you draw.

Glossary of Terms

Befriending
When Self develops a relationship of trust with a part.

Blending
The situation in which a part has taken over your consciousness, so that you feel its feelings, believe its attitudes are true, and act according to its impulses.

Burden
A painful emotion or negative belief about yourself or the world, which a part has taken on as the result of a past harmful situation or relationship, usually from childhood.

Criticized Child
An exile who believes the judgments of the Inner Critic and feels ashamed, worthless, not valuable, guilty, self-doubting, or inadequate. It is both harmed and activated by the Critic.

Defender
A protector that argues with people who judge you and that tries to prove that you are valuable and didn't do anything wrong.

Destroyer
A type of Critic that makes pervasive attacks on your fundamental self-worth. It is deeply shaming and tells you that you shouldn't exist.

Exile
A young child part that is carrying pain from the past.

Guilt Tripper
A type of Critic that attacks you for some specific action you took (or didn't take) in the past that was harmful to someone, especially someone you care about. It might also attack you for violating a deeply held value. It constantly makes you feel that you are bad and do not deserve to be forgiven.

Inner Champion

An aspect of your Self that supports and encourages you and helps you feel good about yourself. It is the magic bullet for dealing with the negative impact of the Inner Critic.

Inner Controller

A type of Critic that tries to control impulsive behavior, such as overeating, getting enraged, using drugs, or engaging in other addictions. It shames you after you binge, use, or act out. It is usually in a constant battle with an impulsive part.

Inner Critic

A protector that judges you, demeans you, and pushes you to do things. It tends to make you feel bad about yourself and limits your capacity to act freely.

Inner Defender

A protector that tries to argue with the Critic and prove that you are worthwhile.

Molder

A type of Critic that tries to get you to fit a certain societal mold or act in a certain way that is based on your own family or cultural mores. It attacks you when you don't fit and praises you when you do.

Part

A subpersonality, which has its own feelings, perceptions, beliefs, motivations, and memories.

Perfectionist

A type of Critic that tries to get you to do everything perfectly. This part has very high standards for behavior, performance, and production. When you don't meet its standards, the Perfectionist attacks you by saying that your work or behavior isn't good enough.

Protector

A part that tries to block off pain that is arising inside you or to protect you from hurtful incidents or distressing relationships in your current life.

Retrieval

The step in the IFS process in which the Self takes an exile out of a harmful childhood situation and into a place where it can be safe and comfortable.

Self

The core aspect of you that is your true self, your spiritual center. The Self is relaxed, open, and accepting of yourself and others. It is curious, compassionate, calm, and interested in connecting with other people and your parts.

Self-Leadership

The situation in which your parts trust you, in Self, to make decisions and take action in your life.

Taskmaster

A type of Critic that tries to get you to work hard in order to be successful. It attacks you and tells you that you are lazy, stupid, or incompetent in order to motivate you. It often gets into a battle with a part that procrastinates in order to avoid work.

Unblending

Separating from a part that is blended with you so that you can be in Self.

Unburdening

The step in the IFS process in which the Self helps an a part to release its burdens through an internal ritual.

Underminer

A type of Critic that tries to undermine your self-confidence and self-esteem so you won't take risks where you might fail or suffer humiliation. It may also try to prevent you from getting too big, powerful, or visible in order to avoid attack or rejection.

Witnessing

The step in the IFS process in which the Self witnesses the childhood origin of a part's burdens.

Resources

Finding an IFS Therapist: The website of the Center for Self-Leadership, the official IFS organization, www.selfleadership.org contains a geographic listing of IFS-certified therapists. Many therapists offer IFS sessions by telephone.

Inner Critic and IFS Classes and Groups: Bonnie Weiss and Jay Earley teach phone and in-person classes for the general public on using IFS to work with the Inner Critic. Visit our website www.personal-growth-programs.com/ or email us bonnieweiss@gmail.com or earley.jay@gmail.com.

Inner Critic Questionnaire and Profiling Program for your Inner Critic and Inner Champion is available at www.psychemaps.com/ or www.personal-growth-programs.com

Books

Freedom From Your Inner Critic: A Self-Therapy Approach, by Jay Earley and Bonnie Weiss. Also the Companion Exercise book can be downloaded free from our website

Activating Your Inner Champion Instead of Your Inner Critic describes the seven types of Inner Critics and allows you to profile your version of them in detail using a web program. Each of the seven has an Inner Champion that is the magic bullet for transforming that particular type of Critic.

Self-Therapy: A Step-by-Step Guide to Creating Wholeness and Healing Your Inner Child Using IFS, by Jay Earley. Shows how to do IFS sessions on your own or with a partner. Also a manual of the IFS method that can be used by therapists. Bonnie has produced a card deck based on the illustrations in this book.

The Pattern System, by Jay Earley, The Pattern System is a systematic approach to understanding personality that can lead directly to psychological healing and personal growth. This book provides an overview of the system for helping professionals, psychologists, and the general public.

Pattern Books. We have published five books that deal with specific patterns from the Pattern System. Each book is connected to a workbook on the web that allows you to actively work with this pattern and develop a practice for changing it and manifesting the healthy capacity in your life. The books are *Embracing Intimacy, Taking Action (Procrastination), Letting Go of Perfectionism , Beyond Caretaking, and A Pleaser No Longer*.

Introduction to the Internal Family System Model, by Richard Schwartz. A basic introduction to parts and IFS for clients and potential clients.

Internal Family Systems Therapy, by Richard Schwartz. The primary professional book on IFS and a must-read for therapists.

The Mosaic Mind: Empowering the Tormented Selves of Child Abuse Survivors, by Richard Schwartz and Regina Goulding. A professional book on using IFS with trauma, especially sexual abuse.

You Are the One You've Been Waiting For: Bringing Courageous Love to Intimate Relationships, by Richard Schwartz. A popular book providing an IFS perspective on intimate relationships.

Audio Products:

Meditations: We have produced meditations to help evoke the **Inner Champions** for all of the inner critics; and mediations for each of the steps of the IFS process. http://www.personal-growth-rograms.com/store/meditations.

Demonstration Sessions: A good selection of demonstration sessions with real clients by Bonnie Weiss and Jay Earley. Examples of work with each of the Inner Critics.
http://www.personal-growth-programs.com/store/demonstration-sessions

Web-Based Resources:

Self-Therapy Journey, Jay Earley. A web application for personal growth and psychological healing based on the Pattern System and IFS. It includes descriptions of psychological issues, stories, checklists, guided journaling, guided meditations, customized reports, and homework practices.

Self-Expressions: A Part Art Gallery a website for anyone interested in sharing artistic expressions of their parts. http://selfexpressionsartgallery.com

Made in the USA
Coppell, TX
29 December 2019